THE KIDS

Hannah Lowe was born in Ilford to an English mother and Jamaican-Chinese father. She has lived in London, Brighton and Santa Cruz, California. She studied American Literature at the University of Sussex and has a Masters degree in Refugee Studies, and a PhD in Creative Writing from Newcastle University. She has worked as a teacher of literature, and is now a lecturer in Creative Writing at Brunel University.

Her pamphlet *The Hitcher* (The Rialto, 2011) was widely praised. Her first book-length collection *Chick* (Bloodaxe Books, 2013) won the 2015 Michael Murphy Memorial Prize, was shortlisted for the Forward Prize for Best First Collection, the Fenton Aldeburgh First Collection Prize and the Seamus Heaney Centre Prize for Poetry, and was selected for the Poetry Book Society's Next Generation Poets 2014 promotion. This was followed by two pamphlets, *R x* (sine wave peak, 2013) and *Ormonde* (Hercules Editions, 2014), and her family memoir *Long Time No See* (Periscope, 2015). She also read from *Long Time, No See* on BBC Radio 4's *Book of the Week* in 2015. Her second full-length collection, *Chan*, was published by Bloodaxe in 2016, followed by a pamphlet, *The Neighbourhood* (Out-Spoken Press) in 2019. Her third full collection, *The Kids* (Bloodaxe Books, 2021), was the Poetry Book Society Choice for Autumn 2021. It won the 2021 Costa Poetry Award, and is shortlisted for the 2021 T.S. Eliot Prize and Costa Book of the Year. She has been poet in residence at Keats House, and in 2020 she received a Cholmondeley Award from the Society of Authors.

HANNAH LOWE

The Kids

BLOODAXE BOOKS

Printed in Great Britain by Bell & Bain Limited, Glasgow, Scotland, on
acid-free paper sourced from mills with FSC chain of custody certification.

CONTENTS

in memory of John Toolan

No, no, let us play, for it is yet day,
And we cannot go to sleep…

WILLIAM BLAKE, 'Nurse's Song'

The White Dog

My father was dead. I rode to work each morning
through Farringdon, down Charterhouse Street
and saw the same white dog – a terrier – licking
a puddle of blood, leaked by the morning meat
the butchers hauled across their backs to Smithfields.
Dead pigs and chickens hung on silver hooks
below my office. Upstairs, I typed and filed –
memos for Shell, BP, shareholder handbooks.

But every time I saw that dog – trotting
with blood in its beard, its eyes gone cloudy blue,
the same thought tap tap tapped my head, a spoon
against a hard-boiled egg. All afternoon
at the photocopier – typing, filing, typing.
He was dead, he was dead. Now what should I do?

I

The Register

That first September, I climbed the blue stone steps,
past Shakespeare's doubtful face, an old mosaic
of Jamaica, and the ruby blot of lips
where last year's girls had kissed the schoolhouse brick.
Now this year's crop pushed past, all clattery-chat,
their first day back – *Whassup? Salaam!* – the Fugees
blaring from someone's phone: *Ready or not...*
And with that old white dog still barking softly

in my head, I walked the sugar-papered hall
and pushed the classroom door to find a sprawl
of teenagers sat waiting, my 're-sitters',
all back to do what they'd already failed.
I took my seat, and called the register
Deniz, Tyrone, Alicia, Chantelle –

Try, Try, Try Again

Why would anyone want to do again
the thing they'd failed? Like a second driving test
or say, Grade 3 recorder? You tried your best
or did you? It was not enough. Try again?
You'd rather watch *The Price Is Right* than practise
your rendition of *The Ugly Duckling*
or argue with your driving teacher, stalling
in a box junction. So when you rip the notice

open, your keen heart pumping, and find a D
or damn, an E, you'd rather pull the sheets
above your head and flick through Instagram
with earphones in, but still you can hear your mum
repeat: *You'll never get a job without it!*
No one will have you, not Tesco's, not Sainsbury's –

Queen Bee

Why did no one warn me about Monique –
kiss-curls and diamanté nails, Queen Bee
who fixed me with a *fuck you* stare, tipped back
her chair-cum-throne, and, as if I couldn't see,
tip-tapped her phone, and when I said to stash it
she gripped it tight, her eyes unblinking green,
her knuckles taut, and when I went to take it,
she snatched it from the air, and so began

our tug o' war, the way that years before
I'd fought Lyn Johnson for a soldering iron
in Physics, after days of searing glares –
a proper girl-fight: face-slaps, yanking hair,
all hiss and claw, which was really about whether Lyn
or me was Queen Bee of the corridor.

The Art of Teaching I

Before I'd learnt the art of teaching wasn't
to have all eyes on me, but on each other,
to unpick a metaphor, or draw a poster
while making sure the chat chat chat chat wasn't
about their spots, or something on *EastEnders*,
I sat behind my desk and talked and talked
like a manic newsreader, while their faces balked
in boredom or horror, and one by one glazed over –

but nervousness would keep my mouth turned on
like a flooding tap, and as I yakked, the vision
of Spud in *Trainspotting* – who loved a dab
of speed and talked the ears off anyone
who'd listen – would pop to mind, and all the dabs
I'd done myself, more dabs than I'd care to mention.

The Art of Teaching II

Boredom hangs like a low cloud in the classroom.
Each page we read is a step up a mountain
in gluey boots. Even the clock-face is pained
and yes, I'm sure now, ticking slower. If gloom
has a sound, it's the voice of Leroy reading
Frankenstein aloud. And if we break
to talk, I know my questions are feeble sparks
that won't ignite my students' barely beating

hearts. There is no volta here, no turn,
just more of the same: the cloud sinking ever lower,
the air damper, yet more rain. And the task
is unchanging, like spending years chasing a monster
you yourself created. Leroy asks
if he can stop reading. I say, for now, he can.

The Art of Teaching III

How to shake a kid from boredom? Squeeze
their names out like a flannel. Swap their chairs
and split the windows for a freezing breeze,
or zap them with a burning teacher-stare
or fling out questions – the whens and wheres and whys –
or make them role-play, or make them make a poster
and give out coveted supplies (the high-
lighters, the guillotine, the laminator)

or study them – what's in their bag, their walk
to school, their grandmother in Tower Hamlets
or Istanbul. Or map the way they talk,
their slang. Write a glossary and call it
Multicultural London English – *mandem,*
wha-gwan, bare good, a'ight, yo whassup fam?

Technology

Suddenly computers,
screens, an electronic pen
so off the cuff,
I'd ping a poem up –
'To Mercy, Pity, Peace and Love'
or a drawing of the Pardoner,
an image of an ivory tusk
or a map –

one that showed
the 'heyday' of the British Empire,
the pale blue sea around
the places half those kids
had sort of come from once,
shaded rich and bloody red.

Sonnet for Vlad

Come sun or rain or snow, I smoked with Vlad,
the guard from Serbia, on our ashy patch
outside the gate. His bear-like body rattled
as he puffed. He loved his son so much,
the love fell out of him – *my Gregor's English*
perfect, not like mine! he said. *Oh, to see*
my boy play football! He shook his head. *I wish*
for him to be professional. They carry

such bags of hope, these kids of immigrants.
I knew it, teaching them, and being half
of one myself. My dad would clutch and scan
my school report, and mouth like prayer the comments;
he'd make me play Ravel, Rachmaninoff
for his gambling pals, as though he wore my hands.

The Only English Kid

When the debate got going on 'Englishness',
I'd pity the only English kid – poor Johnny
in his spotless Reeboks and blue Fred Perry.
He had a voice from history: *Dunno-miss,
Yes-miss, No-miss* – all treacly-cockney,
rag-and-bone – and while the others claimed Poland,
Ghana, Bulgaria, and shook off England
like the wrong team's shirt, John brewed his tea

exclusively on Holloway Road. So when Aasif
mourned the George Cross banner swinging freely
like a warning from his neighbour's roof,
the subway tunnel sprayed with MUSLIM SCUM,
poor John would sit there quietly, looking guilty
for all the awful things he hadn't done.

Notes on a Scandal

In the ruby light in the Odeon, Leicester Square,
Cate Blanchett looms on screen, about to kiss
a schoolboy, her fingers in his spiked black hair.
She's forty-one. He's fifteen, calls her *Miss.*
My class – their heads tipped back and trainers propped
on backs of seats – eat crisps and jelly beans
as the teacher and the schoolboy rock
between the trains, a blur of half-mast jeans

and hot wild hands. And after, in the square,
the movie still plays on the tiny screen
inside my brain; the streets refract in a blur
of yellow light and rain. My boys careen
around me, play confused. *Why* that *film, Miss?*
They're cocky, amused. *But, Miss, do you want* us?

Boy

I didn't teach him. He wasn't one of mine.
He'd catch my eye across the packed canteen
and hold me there – half-bold, half-clandestine
or else I'd watch him from the mezzanine –
he'd raise a hand and wave a little joy
into my day, ignite a little flame.
There were one or two like that: half-boy,
half-man. I didn't even know his name.

Then seven summers later, a festival,
his tent pitched up in woodland, close to mine.
Shirtless in the shadow with sparkly girls –
flowers in their hair like fairy queens.
He bent to light a spliff below their tree
and looked my way – then looked away from me.

Simile

Timothy Winters has ears like bombs and teeth like splinters...

I can't remember when, or which old teacher
chalked Charles Causley's words on the board, glued them
onto my brain, so whenever I need to remember
or explain what 'simile' is, I use that poem –
poor Timothy Winters with his meagre face
though really, all these years, it's Bobbi, a girl
from school that I've been seeing. Bobbi, who'd chase
and kiss any boy with her ragged, gaping smile,

scuttling the asphalt in her too small skirts
and a galaxy of moon-shaped plasters peeling
from her neck and shoulders. Nobody liked her.
But nowadays to think of Bobbi hurts
like a fading bruise you keep on poking.
Bobbi Bonniwell. What happened to her?

The Sixth-form Theatre Trip

This is more like bloody dog-walking than teaching

ANONYMOUS

You've got more dogs than you can count. Big dogs
and small. One badass dog in headphones mooching
up the aisle. A dog who's smuggled in a hot dog.
Two loving dogs, back row, already smooching.
Some dogs are up on haunches, barking. A dog
or two already dozing, heads in paws,
dog-sighing and dreaming. The other theatre-dogs
look down their snouts – a pair of tutting Chow-Chows,

some sloany Poodles in the box. But when
the curtains lift, and your dogs are hypnotised –
their ears like little hoisted sails, the wag
of tails, their shining dog-hearts fling wide open.
They know these words, these lines, memorised
like buried bones. And don't you love your dogs?

Sonnet for the A Level English Literature and Language Poetry Syllabus

all summer term reading poems –
down in the mud

of words, wanting
the kids to hear what I heard –

breaking the poems apart, slapping
their parts to the board –

'I would love ten years
before the flood'

'The world is charged
with the grandeur of god'

'Yet dearly I love you
and would be lov'd fain'

'Batter my heart'
again, again.

Red-handed

And if you set the kids exam practice
then excuse yourself – even for five minutes –
and in the teachers' bathroom, check your texts
or sneak between the stockroom shelving units
to eat a Twix, or bite your hand to keep
from crying, don't expect when you come back
to find twenty pens in motion, and the tap
of erudition flowing, but know how quick

the kids can zip their chat, though leave it hanging
in the air so you can smell it – like those mornings
when you sense that though your five-year-old
is humming by the sink, the air still holds
the shape he made while wobbling on a chair,
his fingers in the jar of jelly bears.

Sonnet for the Punched Pocket

What would I have done without those wallets,
their white polo holes? I collated essays,
session plans with estimated minutes,
some crossed out mid-lesson, rewritten, the way
I've sometimes stood on stage and edited
a poem, feeling, only in saying aloud,
its idle words. I filled those pockets, fed
them into rainbow ring-binders, the loud

clack-snap of steel, before I slotted them
on shelves above my desk, the little tickets
filled out neatly – *Moon on the Tides*; *Poems
From Other Cultures* – as if you could catch and wrap
a poem, what you thought and felt about it,
under plastic – flattened, silenced, trapped.

Pepys

The posh girls came and took a corner table,
all lip gloss and ribbony hair, each with a fan
of starry GCSEs, a summer of youth hostels
in Europe behind them, and the future wide open
to them like a rainbow parasol, or so
I thought. It was Restoration Comedies
and I was reading the class an essay, and though
I'd seen his name, I'd never heard it – *Peppies*,

I said it, *Peppies*, over and over, until
one girl spoke up: *Do you mean Pepys?* she said,
her voice pulled taut as a noose, as if I were the girl
and she the teacher. And what could I have said?
I read on: *Peppies Peppies Peppies* – cool –
cool as the Trickster, ridiculous as the Fool.

Janine

was a Monday-morning-queasy-feeling.
I was never ready for her choice of sting:
the late strut-in, teeth-kissing, rolling eyes,
my protests thwacked away like swatted flies.
Or else the bleat of questions questions questions,
her pinging hand, a jack-in-the-box, a gun
she kept on firing, asking over and over
why we couldn't study *Harry Potter*

or worse, the searing telescopic stare
I winced in as she coiled a lock of hair
around the middle finger shone at me.
And this went on for months, until somebody
said the thing – and finally bought ease:
my dad was half Jamaican, half Chinese –

Janine II

My dad was half Jamaican, half Chinese?
Her question at my office door. Her face
gone softer, searching mine for vestiges
of blackness, as if she'd find a sign, a trace
the more she sought. And when I told her yes,
was some fire put out? It's hard to know
what heat, or presume a heat at all, or guess
the stakes when teachers rarely look like those

they teach. The whiteness of my skin has been
confusion, chaos, agency. Janine
was nicer, after – all *whatssup Miss?* and *hey!*
like neither me nor her remembered Monday's
knackering, spun-out war. She'd dropped her gun.
I'd somehow been excused. I'd been forgiven.

The Unretained

What happened in the end to Luke? So clever,
    so always utterly stoned he walked like weights
        were in his trainers, until his massive 'biftas'
            put voices in his head that made him late,
                then didn't let him out at all. And what
            about Amal, who slept on strangers' sofas,
        pyjamas in her rucksack, eating Kit Kats
for her breakfast? From joker-in-the-corner
    to never-answered phone, to mates-of-mates
        who may or may have not had seen her? What happened
            to Eliot who went to Feltham? And Martha,
                five-months-pregnant, quitting for her boyfriend
            and a flat, my cautions drifting off her
        like confetti as she strutted through the gates?

All Over It

Dwayne's final media project is on graffiti –
I'm all over it, he says. So obviously
you tell him about Dan, your older brother,
years back, spraying one train then another
with a jangling sack of cans he'd robbed
from Homebase and wire-cutters from the shed.
You reminisce: the police, the social worker
sat while Danny tagged the bathroom mirror

then tiptoed down the stairs and out the door.
Mum crying in the kitchen – *how much more?*
She hid his Puma Suedes to keep him in.
He threw a red brick through our window, running
barefoot down the street. You tell Dwayne this
but he's backing out the room, *Yeah, nice one, Miss –*

Sonnet for Rosie

That girl called Rosie, soft-spoken, shyly clever,
always dressed in high-tops, corduroys,
a khaki bomber, and everywhere I saw her,
kissing or holding the hand of a graceful black boy
from the year above, turned out to be
my old professor's daughter. I can't recall
who told me. It doesn't matter. But how clearly
I remember catching a bus to Stamford Hill

to find his flat – short dress, red lips. And lost,
I asked two men in big fur hats, who looked
straight through me, walking on. But I found his door,
and upstairs, talked music, film, ate buttered toast
while a tiny girl called Rosie grabbed my book
and crawled away across his kitchen floor.

Something Sweet

Winter mornings, I'd buy hot chocolate
and the red-haired green-eyed girl who served me
would smile and sometimes hand me it for free
and I'd drink it down and smoke a cigarette
in the park across from college – something sweet
with something bitter. Before I crossed the track,
I tucked away my numb heart in an ice-pack
in my pocket, where it felt cold and wet

and unforgettable – and went and taught
all day, when I didn't care about the theme
of a poem, the shape of a play. Then marking essays
after class, I'd watch the kids roll out
in their rainbow coats and rucksacks, like streams
of paint – so bright I had to look away.

7/7

(i.m. FS)

It's half past eight and my old friend is late for court.
The eastbound platform at Barbican is busy, bathed in dingy light.

Let's freeze her here, at the edge, pressed tight between
a young undertaker, say, and a ballroom dancer, who minutes later

can't save her life. The train is halted half-way out the tunnel
and from three rows back, I can see my pal – long buttery hair

and half her beaky face. She's looking in the wrong direction
like something's going to happen down the passage, two stops on,

at ten to nine, say. She can't hear me shout her name, so let's
for a moment, change the frame, go up the escalator

into July's smug heat: a cycle courier is static, risen from his seat;
the kiosk man a statue with his spread of awful news and sweets.

Across the street, the flats where my friend has left a burning lamp,
a half-made bed. A single drop is midway falling from a rusted tap.

Ricochet

Four boys blew up three tube trains and a bus.
My old pal was stood beside a bomber.
The police shot a man they said had *Mongolian eyes*.
For days, friends searched the hospitals for her.
The wrong man they shot, they shot eleven times.
We'd heard a voicemail, her saying she was fine.

It was summer still when the kids came back.
Muslim boys in Nikes and thobes and skull caps.
Boyish beards that made them look like men.
Her face still flashed up on the television.
Two girls swept down the hall in full black burkas.
Moniza said a police van took her brother.
The papers called the bombers *British-born*.

British-born

And suddenly, new language – 'British-born' –
for kids who grew up on terraces in Leeds
or tower blocks in Bow, and at weekends tied
their bootlaces for footie on the lawn
and went to college to study Sports or Business
or Car Mechanics and spoke with accents thick
as Yorkshire mud or London bullet-quick –
yes blud! and *innit!* – and were as British as

a pack of salt-and-vinegar, and no,
his teacher hadn't noticed him withdrawing
and no, his mother hadn't wondered who
he called at 2 a.m. in the blue-lit bedroom
of their bungalow – despite her scrubbing,
the words aglow on their garden wall: GO HOME.

II

Mr Presley

Teachers' first names were secrets. I knew them all.
Miss Crane was *Lynda*. Mrs Kumachi, *Rose*.
And my teacher, Mr Presley, was plain old *Paul*.
So why one day I called him *Uncle*, and worse,
Uncle Paul, is anyone's guess. The words
just slithered from my lips like a half-sucked sweet
while my classmates sniggered and I heard
that laughter squeeze around me like a trap net

or a draw-string sack. But why, the next week
did Mr Presley take his scissors, and raise
my plait to its jaws? For whose benefit,
for whose applause? I could feel the silver blades
and his hot chortling breath on the back of my neck
as the kids around me chanted *do it do it!*

Mrs Vanuka

On the cold stone floor of the art cupboard
she knelt us down, and her pudgy hands, gold-garrotted,
threw down the buckets. *Dirty girls.*
Let's see you spit. The clip-clunk of her heels,
the door's hard click – and we did, we did, I spat
until my mouth was sore and my tongue was fat,
while beyond the door we heard her talk,
and the tick-tock stab of the angry chalk.

I'd never known how much my own spit stank.
I spat again, again, until my whole mouth ached
and beside me Neshat sniffled and sobbed –
we couldn't remember which of us first gobbed
or what had happened to make us hate each other
and the base of those buckets still barely covered –

Blocks

First I would draw my name in capitals –
H – A – N across the landscape of the paper
then make the letters three-dimensional,
then colour them, the edges always darker
like my name was standing in the sun,
each letter propping up another, and solid
as though made from wood or brick or iron.
I'd add a line for them to stand on, rooted.

In that house of risk – unstable, unwell –
where often I was thrown like a paper jet
downstairs and hit the hard floor of the hall,
sprawled useless as a crumbled alphabet,
those drawings mattered. That name I wrote for myself,
over and over, standing up for itself.

She

She brought me a glass of orange squash each morning
and hers was the strong soothing hand that led me
to school, and left me skipping or hopscotching
in the still-dark playground, while she drank her coffee
in the staff room. Then later, often, I'd see her
scolding some nervy tearful boy in the hall
and I'd repeat in my head *is she my mother?*
hearing her voice come down like the chunky heel

of a boot, stubbing a beetle out.
She is my mother, she is my mother – my mantra
when she grabbed our puppy by his collar
and dragged him from his bed to crush his snout
in whatever bad thing he hadn't meant to do.
My mother? She grabbed me by the collar too.

Bethena

If I asked, she'd put down her cigarettes
or tea towel, and sit on the emerald velvet stool,
and from her hands, tight-knitted hands, the notes
fell out, like gloves unravelling their wool.
She'd play Scott Joplin's waltz *Bethena*, its title
like her name, so I thought the song was hers,
its pining melody, a silk-scarf fall
of crotchets, quavers. That song was in her fingers

like there are songs in mine, though I rarely play –
so little time. But today, I'm listening
to Scott Joplin on my speaker, and thinking
of the green and glacial drawing-room, the way
she played those dying phrases, the grace, the pain.
Betony was my mother's given name.

Étudier

(for Miss Forbes and Sharon Cranmer)

I played the beautiful music of the dead –
waltzes, *études*. Miss Forbes would hold her pencil
and make the faintest marks in her 2B lead.
So particular, her parlour with its sills
of old cracked china and dried camellias.
She said, *if only you would practise more*
and when I did, my hands would sing across
the keys. With her, I learnt what learning was for.

She died. I went to Sharon, who wore black –
embroidered skirts, black lipstick, blue-black hair –
her thin, mercurial hands. In the room upstairs,
I played Debussy – better than before –
but my eye was on the albums leant in stacks
beside the door, *The Smiths, The Clash, The Cure.*

Martin and Pam

Funny to learn it now, his first name: *Martin*.
So man-with-a-lawnmower suburban. So Sundays
in the aisles of B&Q. Not a name for the man
who pelted chalk, and stalked the wood-dark hallways
in Oxford robes that hid the muscle and meat
he let me know was there, the anger flexing
in his hands. He'd snap my name like a belt
then slap the table so I felt the sting.

And Mrs Bradshaw's name was *Pamela*
or *Pam*, as soft as tea and custard creams.
She'd make us run six miles in knickers and vests,
her whistle rudely screaming over frost,
and afterwards she'd watch us in the showers
as we tried to hide our bodies in the steam.

The Only Black Girl

The kids flicked names at her like Ludo counters,
not just for being black, but for living, like I did,
the wrong side of the tracks – no million-quid,
mock-Tudors in Forest Gate or Ilford. *Scrounger,*
jew-girl, sponger. But Natalie was a fighter,
a *whadyou-call-me* poke-and-puncher. She smacked
and shoved her way into a tighter crook –
the office – where a gang of teachers caught her

and that was that. Then later, when some mother-
or-the-other saw my dad parked up,
I caught a blow or two – *oi pick-n-mixer!*
white wog! But I had skin the kids forgot
and none of Natalie's fire: there was no wallop
or slap in the hands I clenched inside my pockets.

Rain Dance

I was twelve in '89, too young for raves
but Danny taped a shrine of crinkly flyers
to his wall: *Rain Dance*, *World Party*, *Fantasia*.
The morning after, his bedroom was a cave
of boys in shadow slouched across the floor.
The reek of ganja, thud of bass – my brother,
cross-legged and shirtless by his record player,
me spying through the hinge-light of his door.

Now I watch old footage: ravers dancing
in a muddy field, a girl with lilac dreadlocks
whose fingers flashed out stars. The boys look like
he used to, heading those giddy summer evenings
when I lay for hours, my head abuzz,
listening for the drums on Rainham Marshes.

The Pitch

On the muddy pulp of the rugby pitch,
he knelt above me, our drunken tongues not kissing
but attacking, our mouths a mushy sandwich,
only breaking out for a swig of gin,
then back to the ground. Was it Jimmy or Steve
who helped me from my blouse? A rubbing paw
below my bra, my arm bent wrong in my sleeve.
Then when I looked across the pitch, I saw

the other girls were scattered on the grass
and the nearest girl, I knew without seeing,
was surrounded by a school of boys
as if she were a dying jellyfish
in the wash of the morning tide. And the smallest boy
with a stick or something like it, prodding, prodding.

John I

Pink Hummingbird

The postcard he sent you in that long wet summer
had, on one side, a pale pink hummingbird
and overleaf, his notes on your essay on Faulkner
in his usual turquoise ink; the words,
you imagined, written in sunlight on the bed
of his book-stuffed flat, each weighed with care
like a love letter, though it was you who wanted
him. All summer, you waited for September:

to be back again in the tattered classroom,
the tables pushed together, and him at the top
like a doting father, or a bridegroom,
or like God, if God wore Doc Marten shoes
and a silver sleeper in one ear – not the God
you didn't believe in, but one who believed in you.

John II

*For Colored Girls Who Have Considered Suicide
When the Rainbow Is Enuf*

Our vowels were flat as the dead fish that floated
in Dagenham Docks, but still John made us
recite these lines meant for black women who said
i have/ poems/ big thighs/ lil tits which made us blush
as our estuary tongues went tripping
over *cuz* and *enuf*, and the slashes the poet
scattered over her page. And the whole bloody thing
might well have been staged on another planet

compared to Essex and my pals, whose mums
served up school dinners, whose dads worked nights at Fords.
We could just make out the half-rubbed words
of last year's kids – *discourse, nationhood* –
and soon I biro'ed in my own new terms:
hegemony, resistance, sisterhood.

Love

Love was the boy I broke up with years ago.
He lived on a grey estate in Upton Heights.
He bought me tins of cider and Marlboro Lights
and sometimes carved my name in fried potatoes
spelled out on my plate. One night he led me
through the streets, past moonlit maisonettes
and tower blocks, to dawn on Wanstead Flats
and as though I were a bride, he made a bed –

his jacket on the grass, and swans in the marshes
white as the pills we swallowed down with lager,
our bodies pressing tight as a new book's pages –
his T-shirt, his hands, his sweat, his tongue, the tower
windows' blinking lights, the lifting sun,
the body doing what it hadn't done.

So Amazing

It's so amazing to be loved
I'd follow you to the moon in the sky above

LUTHER VANDROSS, 'So Amazing'

But god was Shaun Escoffery, aged twenty,
on the college stage singing *So Amazing*
and looking down, I still believe, at me.
His voice was like a shirt unbuttoning,
hot palms on skin. And what is prayer but praise
and quiet entreaty? Below my breath, I said
a prayer for him; for Shaun, whose singing raised
a gale in me, but whose beautiful shaved head

was full of a formal God and the Pentecostals
who told him to deny the flesh, deny
the glittering desires of teenage girls.
I knew nothing about men or sex or love
but at night, my palm between my thighs,
he sailed me to the moon in the sky above.

The Stroke

For days after the stroke, she lay bed-bound,
misdiagnosed – the Doctor said 'Bell's palsy'
of her weeping eye and tilted frown, her hand
cold-numb below the eiderdown. The telly
in the corner spun blue-light, an anarchy
of voices. My father, dying himself and lost,
brought trays of tea and plates of buttered toast.

Outside, September shook the leaves down, steered
a chain of infants to their turquoise pegs
to hang their anoraks and wait for her,
small bodies on the story mat, cross-legged.
For thirty-seven years, the autumns leap-frogged,
time forward-rolling on. Strangers stopped her
on the high street, *hello miss, it's me, remember?*

Inside, she heard the freight trains jogging past.
My father shuffled room to room, and phoned me,
which he'd never done, and whispering, asked
if I would come? I didn't listen to the worry
on his tongue – old friends from university
sat huddled at my kitchen bench, late supper,
the night's dénouement – shots of flamed Sambuca

with coffee beans for health, happiness,
prosperity... I remember her body, glistening
in the bath, the rolls of belly, each one pressed
against the other, licked by water and her skin,
her veins, blue flowering on porcelain,
in the small blue bathroom with its frosted window
and rusted taps, a coral print kimono

hanging on its hook, its purple ribbon ties
and through the open door, I hid and watched her –
the secret breasts and stomach, groin and thighs,
the way all daughters must survey their mothers.
Her body was a blueprint, harbinger
of duty, worry, pain. Downstairs, my Nan
smoked roll-ups, waiting to be waited on.

I didn't go. Until I did. Some arrangement
for dad to drive and pick me up one night.
By the sign for Upney Tube, gas-blue fluorescent,
I waited, waited, until an hour late,
I dialled home in the blunt and pissy light
of the payphone on the hill, that slope between
the streets where I grew up, and the A13

        where industry began – black factories,
        the dirt-blue river, sewage works and gas drums,
        the toxic heaps of Beckton Alps, old grease
        and slag and stone. Above the traffic thrum
        I heard her lift the telephone, said *Mum,*
        it's me, and the breath I heard I knew was hers
        but when I spoke again she didn't answer

        and when I spoke again, she couldn't speak.
        Young commuters pushed the station turnstiles,
        raised umbrellas, rushed off into the dark
        and still my mother didn't answer. Rain nailed
        the phone-box, dashes hardening to hail,
        and I was shouting at her, shouting *Where is he?*
        Why can't you hear me, Mum? Why can't you hear me?

My dad pulled in, a blur behind his wipers,
just lost or late, and then as I was hanging up
she spoke a word or two I couldn't hear
but her voice was formal, small, like she was high-up
in a building with an office at the top
with little windows, in a city she didn't know,
in a cold blue country a hundred years ago.

At home, she wore a too-small yellow jumper,
laid foetal on the sofa to the telly's
constant upbeat chatter. I cooked them dinner,
mopped the spills. And when she looked at me
I was teacher now, and mother. Reluctantly
I took the broom, the duster, the Mr Sheen,
the mop, the bleach. And I began to clean.

Sonnet for Noah

My father died that winter. And each man after
was a patch I stitched onto my heart.
Across the lecture theatre – goofy-smart,
ripped jeans, a fisherman's jumper, much older
than me, of course. He worked with refugees.
In class, we studied asylum, displacement, borders
though I was only looking for my father
in those books I crammed like remedies

for loss. He had a flat in Finsbury.
I couldn't find it now, though many times
I've wanted to. The sea-blue bathroom, tiny
as a womb. The rusted tub where I reclined
between his sudsy knees and kept afloat –
Noah behind me, solid as a lifeboat.

Welling

1993

On the news that night they called us violent youth
but what I remember is the green cord jacket I was wearing
pulled from a bargain bin that morning
and a busload of us singing our way down South,
the yellow placards like a bobbing sea of lollipops,
a beautiful man with dreadlocks, studs in his chin
and us on the frontline, marching and chanting
until the chanting suddenly stopped,

then one voice shouted *Police protect the Nazis!*
the police like a wall of giant flies, their graceful white horses,
then silence – no moment in my life do I remember quieter –
before the charges, the bricks, the screams,
two boys with gashed heads running together,
that animal smell, red smoke, blood on my sleeves –

Dear Professor

I wanted to be the ashtray in your office, the ash,
the slim cigarette you bit between your teeth, the flash

of smoke thrown from your mouth in laughter, the students
you smoked with in secret, talking books the way my parents

talked money or *EastEnders* or MOTs; I wanted
to wear green and dye my hair your bloody shade of red

and sit in the courtyard with coffee and that bright regal look,
to have a glamorous name, a desk, so many books,

to be pushed the way you pushed me, 'for god's sake, *think*',
to have a brain and use it, to be paid to think.

Years later, in a checkout queue, the woman waiting
was an echo of you – your face reeled in, hands scattering

coins across the floor. When I helped you from your knees,
it was love, I wanted the words on my lips. *Karina. Please.*

White Roses

The boys from Dobbins show me photographs –
a greenhouse full of old syringes, a lift
graffitied in sick and rusty blood. The laugh
about the leaking stove they had to shift –
how a hundred mice came rushing, a rug
of mice unrolling, and the house of two rich ladies,
its sinks flooded with pee, the glued-in plugs,
their window-sills gone marmitey with flies.

We've seen it all, they smile, *so this is nothing*.
And while one kneels to scrape away the slag
of my mother's kitchen, the other stuffs the bin-bags –
shoes shoes shoes. I pull her mattress out
and find the ring she said was stolen; a fort
of crumpled tissues, white roses wet with crying.

Daughter

My daughter is quiet, so quiet I sometimes wonder
jf she's there at all. The only time she speaks
is when I tuck her in, her sugary whisper
in my ear – asks me if her brother's asleep.
Can't let herself go down, until she knows
he's sunk below the slumber ground. Sometimes
I do her plaits, and loop them on her pillows,
two adder snakes to guard her. I can't tame

her brother. In the morning, before I wake
she combs them out in mermaid waves. She waits
for me to come, her bed a sea rock in the sea,
her legs a coiled-up fishtail in the sheets.
When I go to speak, she turns away,
dives down, and swiftly swims away from me.

House

This poem is like a house where I once lived.
Upstairs, four rooms where everyone I loved
lay and dreamt their solitary dreams,
the sound of crying in the turquoise bathroom,
the tap's fat drip. Above our heads, an attic
with a splintered window, spongy dust, bare brick,
a battered trunk that held an ocean,
another of shame, and from the rafters,
rain and rain and rain.
        Downstairs, a different weather –
four muggy rooms, the telly's sunny blether,
a technicolor garden. I hopped the path
on my red space hopper, and raised my hand
to wave at a girl who looked like me, upstairs,
her hands and face pressed tightly to the glass.

The River

Not another poem about my father,
as though he's been forever running through me,
rising, churning, like the Yallahs River
where he was born. That river flooded yearly
so no one could cross. What have I learnt after
all these years of loss? At poetry readings
I perform him, hope for sighs or laughter.
I paint him at casino tables, cooking

Chinese suppers, lying in the spare room, dying.
I want applause, but see the real man standing
at the door. There's something he wants to say.
And nothing's been forgiven. Then I hear
the water rushing down the corridor.
He's swimming hard – but it carries him away.

Players

My parents taught me smoking. The midnight nip
to the Esso garage for twenty Players,
the kitchen-table vigil, lighting one tip
from another, then another. No matches or lighter?
They bent to the cooker's flame. No credit, no cash?
My dad would search the bin to twist tobacco
from dog-ends, squeeze it, suck it in. Or flush?
They'd pile nine, ten black boxes on the bureau –

small coffins in a stack. Stained walls, grey fug,
the constant tweezering of fags, that plug
between the lips. It took me years to stop.
Though still some lonely nights I spark one up
and that red light in the darkness leads me back
to where they're waiting, holding out the pack.

III

There was a pudding in the bed
This is what the pudding said
There was a pudding in the bed
This is what he said:

Pour some custard on me now!
Pour some custard on me now?
Pour some custard on me now!
All over my head!

SONG MADE FOR RORY

The Sky Is Snowing

The sky is snowing, Rory, and overnight
the earth's been eiderdowned in feather-white.
Today is Story Day, but the schools are shut –
the playground through the rails is a bassinet
of silent snow. No Burglar Bill will go
to school today, no Alice or Gruffalo.
On the news, a garter snake of cars
has slept the night below the frozen stars.

The sky is snowing, love, in pale marshmallows
and flecks of mint. You're at the kitchen window
in your burglar stripes and mask and bag
of swag. My little crooked scallywag.
Let's lift the window open, just a slip,
and catch this snowstorm on your fingertip.

Skirting

Rory rides these streets in his battered pram
like a prophet, his milky arms spread open,
face first into the world. So all things come:
all breeds of dog, the hips of postmen, policemen,
joggers, lunatics, dead leaves, silk rain,
sad toddlers in their own worn cars. He holds
the men off too – you see that nice young man
bowling towards us, snug-jeaned and smiling, bold

as brass? He couldn't touch me if he wanted,
my lad would keep him back – my cavalier
in corduroy and a bobble hat. He's chalked
a magic ring, a Mum-and-Rorysphere.
So all the fellows skirt us, dodge his slap,
but my own small fellow loves me. Yes, there's that.

Scooting

My Rory wants to scoot on his own, dammit,
to soar one-footed down the street – who cares
about red lights or buses or reckless cars?
You cars should watch it, else he'll mount your bonnet
and flick his wheels until his scooter whirls
like a helicopter-blade on your old tin roof,
might even lift you, levitate a troupe
of cars into the sky, while boys and girls

look up, and wave, call out their *toodle-oos!*
or kneel to aim their finger-guns. And when
you cars combust, a million curlicues
of car-dust will decorate the sky and spin
around my boy, scooting on his own
between the stars and planets, across the moon.

Fire Scissors Drowning

Each night before I sleep
the boy climbs the railings of the balcony,
laughing and fearless,
one hand pointing to a star
and out he steps into the thin black air

or even lying here in the Algarve sun, watching
the green sea, crisp as glass,
I see his father running from the cliffs,
the boy bloody and limp
in his arms

Kathryn says we all have our special
fears – fire, scissors, drowning – yes,
ever since that boy was born,
he's been falling.

The Size of Him

Rory's on the sofa sobbing, tucked in the nook of his dad's blue jumper
because the boy next door, all toddler ego, has pelted him with Lego

then balls, as Ror took cover, then next-door's mocked him for crying.
I scoop him up, though I can nearly-not lift him – *so tall!* the librarian says –

he's four in seven-year-old's trousers. *Look at the size of him!* the checkout girl
half-screams like he's a prize turkey. She thinks he's still a baby.

He's still weeping, big bare feet locked behind me. He wants *Dr Who*,
a show his dad loves, show he wants to watch but doesn't understand.

I snuck downstairs to watch it with my brother. By 13, he was bait
for the bullies good and proper – 6′4 with duct-tape on his glasses,

soon throwing punches – breakfast rages, fist to the mirror,
a brick through our own front door. Now the Daleks – *exterminate, exterminate!* –

roll towards the camera. Rory's laughing-scared. He's climbing
his dad's shoulders, sliding down his back, to hide while he still can.

Sonnet for Boredom

Some days it's all he talks of – Minecraft, Minecraft –
world I won't set foot in: skeletons
and zombies, mooshrooms, lava? When he's gone,
he's gone for hours, and the iPad is a raft
he sails from breakfast to lunch on, lunch to dinner,
though I try to haul him in – the park in rain
or drawing, baking – nothing's easier
than giving in. When I was six, my game

was boredom. Bored, lying on the floor
of my bedroom, hoping for the phone to ring,
unpicking stickers to stick them down again,
wishing for a tiny secret door
below the bed, for the curtain elves and gnomes
to stand on toadstools, whispering my name.

Balloons

These five-year-olds remind me of the balloons
we had one summer: heart-shaped helium,
in rainbow colours; we pushed notes inside them
and let them go, believing that the moon
might catch those small hearts climbing up the sky.
I watch these children knelt around their teacher,
their small hands shooting high to give an answer,
any answer, just the chance to try.

But the kids I taught, who came to me at the edge
of childhood – was it really, then, too late?
In the common room we said it only took
one class, one hour, to know the grades they'd get,
as though there were a Magic 8 Ball, wedged
at one conclusion, no matter how hard you shook.

In H&M

I've seen her fifty times, tidying the earrings
or punching the till. The same long rainbow hair
she had at school. Then one time, as I'm paying
I say *I used to teach you, remember?* She stares,
then frowns. Looks down at her hands, smoothing a fold.
It's Hannah. She says nothing. Except her look's
not happy. More scared. *I wasn't very good.*
She holds out my shopping bag. *I can't do books.*

I'm in there often. The store's around the corner.
I see her wheeling clothes rails, making piles
of jumpers, colour-ordered – red, gold, brown.
She's diligent. And funny. People like her,
I can tell. Sometimes I wave or smile –
then the shutters of her face come down.

Sonnet for Darren

Men don't look at me like this anymore –
the way this tall young man is looking at me.
I feel my heart swing open like a door.
The traffic lights flash red. Rory, just three,
rolls backwards and forwards on his tricycle.
The man's still looking, yes, at *me*, his smile
like heaven. I remember this: trouble,
desire, bliss, but god, it's been a while

and here he is, so close I can smell his skin.
White t-shirt gleaming. His afro flamed like sunbeams
around his face, which is lovely, like a dream
I used to have. And now his mouth is moving,
saying *Miss, it's me, Darren, remember?*

We chat. Lights change. Rory and I cross over.

Zoom

And who else had a Zoom date with a total stranger
and brashly said *I like being told what to do*
to which he said *Come over* – so caught an Uber
through deserted streets, while the virus still flew
on the air like lethal amoeba? Before him kissing
your nipples and fucking you, a hand clamped over
your mouth, he knelt at your feet in the shower, asking
to be peed on. You'd been there, what, an hour?

Weeks later, recounting to your friends on screen,
wondering if after the baby, the seven years
of being good, the shoulds and could-have-beens,
you're basically the same loose cannon, firing
yourself in all directions. They say *Stop crying.*
It's why we love you. You nod. Hold back the tears.

Aretha in the Bath

'Precious Lord, Take My Hand', she's singing
from your portable speaker, and the water,
hot as you can stand, opens up your skin
to let her voice in, and the preacher, the choir,
the Hammond organ's rising call. Who'd doubt
this kind of faith? *'I'll be there, yes I will.'*
The music floats you, turns you inside out,
liquefying as a sleeping pill

so you feel yourself – not your body's hunger
for the lido's wintery water, but the water
itself; not the lonely woman who waits
at the window, wanting a stranger's kiss
on her shoulder, but her blue delphinium dress,
a hundred flowers pooling at her feet.

His Books

He still hasn't taken his books. Each morning
I wake to the rows of spines – Burns, Pessoa,
HD, the lyrics of Dylan. A delicate rainbow
of manuscripts. Even now I see him reading,
leant on a pillow, drafts by his friends, the writers
of Scotland. And there's a single photograph:
him as a boy in the rain on a highland path,
cloaked in a yellow mac, stood with his father.

He'll pick them up next week. Then I'll spread
my books across, fill up the empty shelves,
the way for eight months now I've stretched myself
across the new terrain of this huge white bed.
I stay up reading late – poems, poems.
Then in the dim gold light, I write about him.

Anjali Mudra

(for Richard Price)

Thank you, Richard, for everything you've taught me –
the hand-stitched book, the heft of vellum paper,
the folded poem, the engraved poem, the poetry
of Edwin Morgan. Delicacy, desire,
language. I wanted your care for letters, your care
for history, tradition, outside tradition,
the wild white beach at Mellon, Burns Night prayer,
to make a grand and persevering passion.

Today's our son's birthday. Soon we'll live apart,
him half the time with you, and half with me.
What better symbol of a broken heart?
But in yoga, Luana says to place somebody
in our heart-centre. I close my hands in prayer,
give thanks. *Anjali Mudra*. I seal you there.

Sonnet for Rory with Soap Bubbles

These hot summer nights, my boy wants milk,
to call out *Mum Mum Mum* again and again.
While I'm reading essays by the fan,
I hear him in the bathroom, his secret talk
to the running tap. I find him balancing
a handful of bubbles back to bed. It is
so hot, and why have the birds stopped singing
darling? Who can sleep on a night like this?

And how will it hurt him, now we've broken up,
his dad and me? How will we be? So I let
my son get up to pump the sea-blue soap
and walk the suds he loves so much to bed.
Then finally he sleeps among the foam,
a fizzing bomb of bubbles in his palm.

Nǐ hǎo

In bed this morning, reading Adrienne Rich,
Rory beside me watching a lime green monster
called Muzzy on his iPad. Muzzy is teaching
my son Chinese. *Nǐ hǎo*, the boy says, over
and over. Outside the birds have been saying hello
for hours, and the early sky has finally bloomed
to blue. Someone somewhere playing a piano.
Every man I bring into this bedroom

says *Books!* regarding the shelves, the jamboree
of books in every colour, stacked two rows thick,
who knows how many words, not all of them read.
But this April morning, it's *Diving into the Wreck*
and I think, is this what aloneness is? A warm bed,
my books, this small boy flowering beside me?